THIS JOURNAL BELONGS TO

_____

D0088712

At the beach,
LIFE IS DIFFERENT.
TIME DOESN'T MOVE
HOUR TO HOUR
BUT
MOOD TO MOMENT.
WE LIVE BY THE CURRENTS,
PLAN BY THE TIDES and
follow the Sun.
—UNKNOWN

THE SEA,

ONCE IT CASTS its SPELL,
HOLDS one IN ITS
NET of WONDER
FOREVER.

—JACQUES–YVES COUSTEAU

THE OCEAN
STIRS *the* HEART,
INSPIRES THE
IMAGINATION &
BRINGS ETERNAL JOY
TO THE SOUL.
-WYLAND

When you walk
on the BEACH at NIGHT,
YOU CAN SAY THINGS YOU CAN'T
SAY IN REAL LIFE.

—JENNY HAN

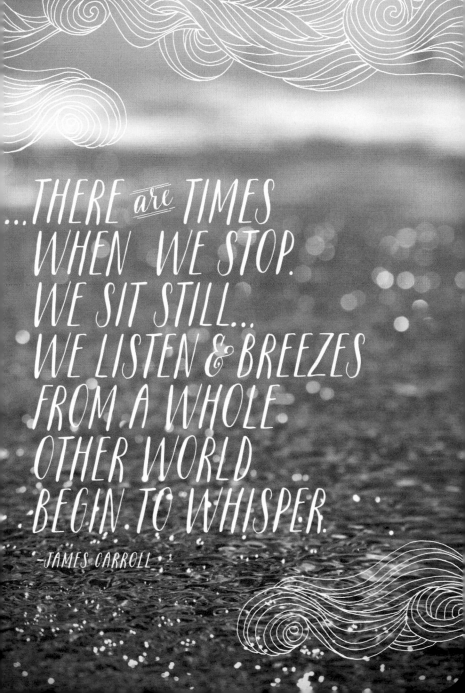

...THERE are TIMES
WHEN WE STOP.
WE SIT STILL...
WE LISTEN & BREEZES
FROM A WHOLE
OTHER WORLD
BEGIN TO WHISPER.

—JAMES CARROLL

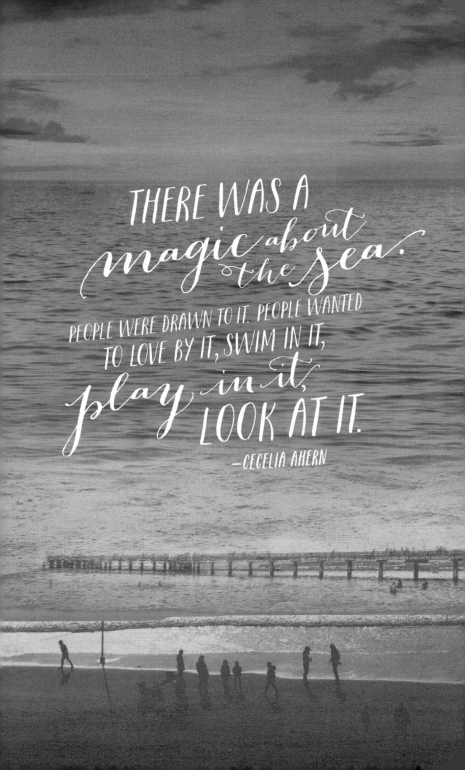

THERE WAS A
magic about the sea.

PEOPLE WERE DRAWN TO IT. PEOPLE WANTED
TO LOVE BY IT, SWIM IN IT,
play in it,
LOOK AT IT.

—CECELIA AHERN

YOU CAN *fall* IN

LOVE

AT FIRST SIGHT WITH A

PLACE

AS WELL AS A *person*.

−ALEC WAUGH

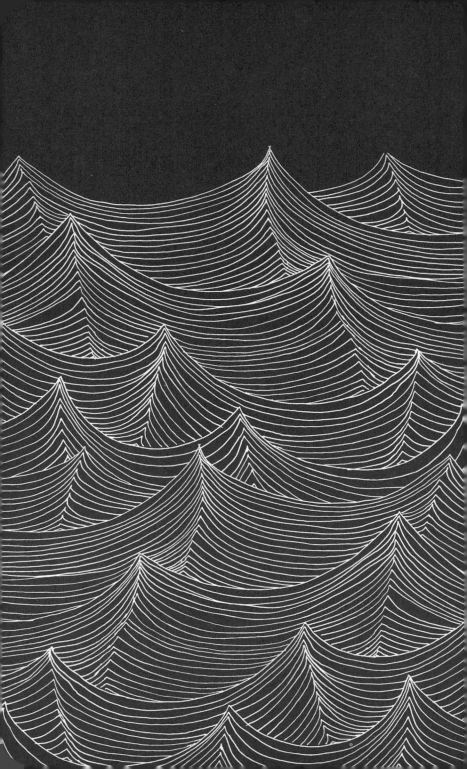

THE VOICE ·of the sea· SPEAKS to the SOUL.

- KATE CHOPIN